SPIDERS

BLACK WIDOW SPIDERS

James E. Gerholdt

ABDO & Daughters

Published by Abdo & Daughters, 4940 Viking Drive, Suite 622, Edina, Minnesota 55435.

Library bound edition distributed by Rockbottom Books, Pentagon Tower, P.O. Box 36036, Minneapolis, Minnesota 55435.

Printed in the United States.

Cover Photo credit: Peter Arnold, Inc.
Interior Photo credits: Peter Arnold, Inc. pages 5, 7, 9, 13, 15, 21
James Gerholdt pages 11, 17, 19
Photos courtesy of Spineless Wonders pages 11, 19

Edited by Julie Berg

Library of Congress Cataloging-in-Publication Data

Gerholdt, James E., 1943
        Black widow spiders / James E. Gerholdt.
        p. cm. — (Spiders)
Includes bibliographical references and index.
        ISBN 1-56239-511-4
1. Black widow spider—Juvenile literature. [1. Black widow spider. 2. Spiders.] I.
Title. II. Series: Gerholdt, James E., 1943- Spiders.
QL458.42.T54G47   1995
595.4'4—dc20   95-17576
                                                                        CIP
                                                                        AC

About the Author
Jim Gerholdt has been studying reptiles and amphibians for more than 40 years. He has presented lectures and displays throughout the state of Minnesota for 9 years. He is a founding member of the Minnesota Herpetological Society and is active in conservation issues involving reptiles and amphibians in India and Aruba, as well as Minnesota.

Contents

BLACK WIDOWS

Black widows belong to one of the 84 spider families called the cobweb weavers.

A spider is an **arachnid**. It has two body parts and eight legs. All arachnids are **arthropods**. Their skeletons are on the outside of their bodies. Spiders are also **ectothermic**. They get their body temperature from the **environment**.

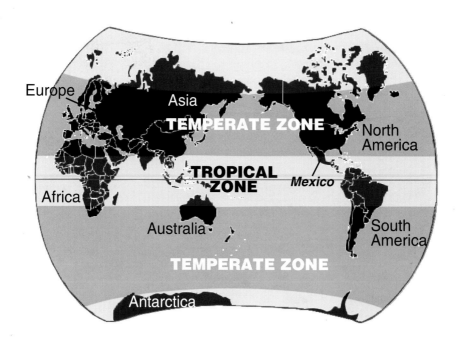

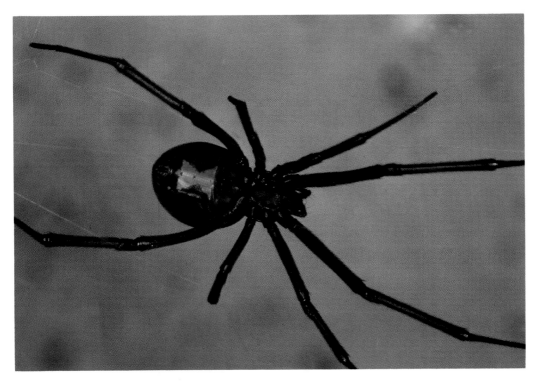

A female black widow found in Arizona.

There are about 37,000 **species** of spiders in the world. More than 2,000 of these are cobweb weavers. More than 230 species are found north of Mexico, five of which are widows. Other widows are found throughout the warm regions of the world.

SIZES

Widows are the largest of the cobweb weavers. The females are one-half (1.2 cm) to six-tenths of an inch (1.5 cm) in length. The males are about one-half this size.

The black widow is one of the smaller widows. The female measures about three-eighths of an inch (9.5 mm). The male black widow is only one-eighth of an inch (3 mm) long.

Male black widows are much smaller than the females.

SHAPES

All black widows have two body parts. The head and **thorax** make up the front body part, called the **cephalothorax**.

The rear body part is called the **abdomen**. This is where the **spinnerets** are found. These spinnerets make the spider's silk.

The male widow has a slender abdomen. The female has a large round abdomen.

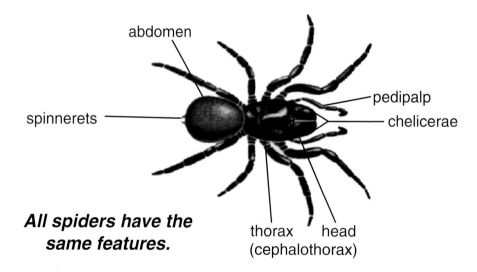

abdomen

spinnerets

pedipalp

chelicerae

thorax   head
(cephalothorax)

***All spiders have the
same features.***

All black widows have two body parts, the cephalothorax and the abdomen.

There are eight long legs attached to the front of the body. The male has longer legs than the female.

Spiders also have a pair of **pedipalps**, which are used to grab **prey**. The two fangs are attached to the **chelicerae**.

COLORS

A female black widow is mostly black in color. She has a bright red hourglass marking on the underside of her **abdomen** that is easy to see. The male is brown in color, with white and reddish markings on the side of the abdomen.

The Mediterranean widow has a series of red markings on the top and sides of its abdomen. The red widow from Florida has red legs and a black abdomen with reddish spots circled with white.

The bright red hourglass is easy to see on this female black widow.

WHERE THEY LIVE

Black widows are found in many different **habitats**. They are common, but stay hidden most of the time. Black widows are found in trash piles, fallen branches, basements, outhouses, garden sheds, and any dark corner where it is quiet.

The females spin an irregular web. The web's silk comes from the spider's **spinnerets**. The silk is very strong and sticky. Any insect that touches the web cannot escape. The spider spends most of its time hanging upside down on the web.

The female spins an irregular web. This is the reason black widows are known as "cobweb weavers."

SENSES

Black widows have the same five senses as humans. Like most spiders, they have eight eyes. But their eyesight is not very good, especially in the male.

Feeling **vibrations** is the spider's most important sense. As the black widow hangs upside down, it can feel when something touches the web.

Black widows can also taste the world around them with the ends of the **pedipalps** and legs.

As it hangs upside down, a black widow can feel when something touches the web.

DEFENSE

The black widow's best defense against enemies is to stay hidden. A female widow will often spin her web in a dark, out-of-the-way place. If she is bothered, she will try to escape. If she can't, she will bite (only the females bite).

Because her bite is poisonous, it is dangerous. The black widow's **venom** can cause a human to stop breathing. An **antidote** can treat this bite.

The venom of the female black widow is very poisonous and may cause a human to stop breathing.

FOOD

Black widows eat insects that become trapped in their web. The web's silk is very strong and sticky. When an insect touches the web, it gets caught. Feeling the **vibrations** from the **prey**, the spider will approach the victim and spin more silk around it.

Once the victim has been wrapped up, it is bitten and killed by the spider's **venom**. Even large insects can be caught and killed. Once the prey dies, the spider sucks out the body fluids.

A cricket has been wrapped in silk and killed by the black widow.

BABIES

All widows hatch from eggs that have been laid by the female. They are laid in an egg case that she has made for them.

The shape of the egg case depends on the **species**. The black widow has a round case that is white or cream colored. She will guard this egg case against any enemy that might threaten it. Often, several egg cases are made during the summer.

Once the baby spiders have hatched, they soon go their own way. Sometimes the female widow will eat the male after **mating**. This is why she is called a black widow.

A female black widow about to lay eggs.

GLOSSARY

Abdomen (AB-doe-men) - The rear body part of an arachnid.

Antidote (ANN-tuh-dote) - A medicine that reverses the effects of a poison.

Arachnid (uh-RACK-nid) - An arthropod with two body parts and eight legs.

Arthropod (ARTH-row-pod) - An animal with its skeleton on the outside of its body.

Cephalothorax (seff-uh-low-THOR-ax) - The front body part of an arachnid including the head and the thorax.

Chelicerae (kel-ISS-err-eye) - The leg-like organs of a spider that have the fangs attached to them.

Ectothermic (ek-toe-THERM-ik) - Regulating body temperature from an outside source.

Environment (en-VI-ron-ment) - Surroundings in which an animal lives.

Family (FAM-i-lee) - A grouping of animals.

Habitat (HAB-uh-tat) - An area in which an animal lives.

Mating - To reproduce young.

Pedipalps (PED-uh-palps) - The two long sense organs on the head of an arachnid.

Prey - Animals that are eaten by other animals.

Species (SPEE-seas) - A kind or type.

Spinnerets (spin-ur-ETTS) - The two body parts attached to the abdomen of a spider where the silk is made.

Thorax (THORE-axe) - Part of the front body part of an arachnid.

Venom - Poison the spider makes and uses to kill its prey.

Vibration (vi-BRAY-shun) - A quivering or trembling motion.

Index

BIBLIOGRAPHY

de Vosjoli, Philippe. *Arachnomania - The General Care and Maintenance of Tarantulas and Scorpions.* Advanced Vivarium Systems, 1991.

Levi, Herbert W. and Lorna R. *Spiders and Their Kin.* Golden Press, 1990.

O'Toole, Christopher (editor). *The Encyclopedia of Insects.* Facts On File, Inc., 1986.

Preston-Mafham, Rod and Ken. *Spiders of the World.* Facts On File, Inc., 1984.

Webb, Ann. *The Proper Care of Tarantulas.* T.F.H. Publications, Inc., 1992.